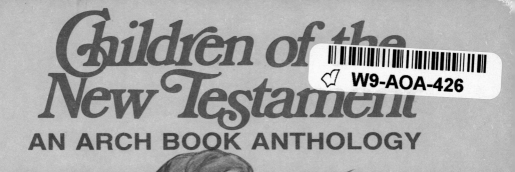

Children of the New Testament

AN ARCH BOOK ANTHOLOGY

CHILDREN OF THE NEW TESTAMENT: An Arch Book Anthology

Copyright © 1986 Concordia Publishing House
3558 S. Jefferson Avenue, St. Louis, MO 63118-3968
Manufactured in the United States of America

From
YOUNG JESUS IN THE TEMPLE   Concordia Publishing House © 1986
    Originally THE BOY WHO WAS LOST
                     Concordia Publishing House © 1972
JON AND THE LITTLE LOST LAMB   Concordia Publishing House © 1965
THE DAY THE LITTLE CHILDREN CAME
                     Concordia Publishing House © 1975
THE BOY WHO GAVE HIS LUNCH AWAY
                     Concordia Publishing House © 1965
THE LITTLE SLEEPING BEAUTY   Concordia Publishing House © 1969

Library of Congress Cataloging in Publication Data

Main entry under title:
    Children of the New Testament.

    Contents: Young Jesus in the temple / by Alyce Bergey—John and the little lost lamb / by Jane Latourette—The day the little children came / by Anne Jennings—[etc.]
    1. Children in the Bible—Biography—Juvenile literature. 2. Bible. N.T.—Biography—Juvenile literature. [1. Children in the Bible. 2. Bible. N.T.—Biography]
BS2446.C44 1986   225.9′505 [920]   85-17122
ISBN 0-570-06206-3

---

1 2 3 4 5 6 7 8 9 10 PP 95 94 93 92 91 90 89 88 87 86

Young Jesus in the Temple

Luke 2:41-52 for children

Written by Alyce Bergey
Illustrated by Betty Wind

Former title: The Boy Who Was Lost

ARCH BOOKS

Copyright © 1972, 1986 CONCORDIA PUBLISHING HOUSE
3558 S. JEFFERSON AVENUE, ST. LOUIS, MO 63118-3968
MANUFACTURED IN THE UNITED STATES OF AMERICA

ISBN 0-570-06203-9

Bright flowers bloomed in Nazareth.
Sweet birds sang everywhere.
Soft breezes blew as Jesus combed
the donkey's coat with care.

His friend, Tobias, wandered by.
"Hi, Toby!" Jesus called.
"Passover's here and this year we
can go — we're twelve years old!
We'll see the temple and other things.
Tomorrow is the day
we all start for Jerusalem —
a hundred miles away!"

Next morning early Jesus helped
tie bundles of supplies
upon the little donkey's back,

and then neath sunny skies,
with all the other families,
they started up the road.

Young Jesus proudly led the small gray donkey with its load.

Clippety-clop! The donkey train moved slowly on its way.
The people sang and talked as on they marched.

At last one day —

"Look! I can see Jerusalem!"
cried Jesus in delight.

They soon were there.
The wide-eyed boys
looked round at every sight:

the towers tall, the golden gate,
the city's high stone walls,

the crowds of people
in the streets,
the bright,
gay market stalls.

"Look, Jesus!" Toby said.
"Up there!
The great
white temple! See?"
"Look at the shining
golden roof!"
cried Jesus
happily.

Then Joseph found an inn.
The great
Passover feast began.
With merry hearts
the family ate
unleavened bread and lamb.

"Passover tells us of the night
God set our people free
by His great love," said Joseph. Then
they all sang joyfully.

In big Jerusalem
there were
so many things to see.
But most of all,
the temple was
where Jesus liked to be.
He liked to hear
the teachers there,
all old and very wise.
He'd listen,
sitting at their feet,
with bright and eager eyes.

When Jesus asked
them questions, all
the teachers were amazed!
"How can a young
lad know so much?"
they said with
eyebrows raised.

The people stayed a week. And then,
one morning bright and clear,
they started back toward Nazareth.

But as the night drew near,
"Where's Jesus?" Joseph asked his wife.
"I don't know!" she replied.
"He must be with the other boys."

She called His name and cried.
No answer came! They quickly went
and found the other lads.
"Have you seen Jesus?"
Joseph asked.
Not any of them had!

They looked and looked for Jesus
and soon became quite worried.
"He isn't here!" they cried. Back to
Jerusalem they hurried!

The next day in the city streets
and at each market stall
they both asked: "Tell us, have you seen
a boy – about so tall?"

"His name is Jesus. He's my son.
We lost Him!" Mary said.
But one by one the merchants and
the strangers shook their heads.

They hurried to the inn where they had stayed when they were there. They cried, "We can't find Jesus! Have you seen Him anywhere?"

But NO one had seen Jesus! And now Mary was alarmed. "What's happened to my son?" she cried. "Oh, maybe He's been harmed!"

Three days had passed. Said Joseph then,
"I know where He might be!
He loved God's house. He could be there."
They quickly ran to see.

When they had reached
the temple church,
they were surprised
and glad!
For there among
the teachers sat
just one young,
bright-eyed lad.

Around Him
many people stood,
all listening in surprise.
"Look!" Joseph said.
"It's Jesus with
the teachers
great and wise!"

Then Jesus' mother went to Him.
Her heart was full of joy,
but scolding just a bit, she said,
"We were alarmed, my Boy!

"We looked all over for You, Son.
Oh, why did You stay here?
We thought that You were lost!" she said
and wiped away a tear.

But gently Jesus said to them,
"Why did you look for Me?
Didn't you know My Father's house
is where I'd surely be?"

They didn't understand His words.
But Mary smiled, and then
the three of them went down the road
to Nazareth again.

The Boy obeyed His parents, and
as years passed one by one,
He grew and learned still more.
How pleased God was with His dear Son!

DEAR PARENTS:

In so many ways Jesus was a regular boy as He was growing up in Nazareth. He had all the usual experiences of a happy childhood. Mary and Joseph couldn't have asked for a better child.

But in one respect the boy Jesus was unusual. He was closely tied, in thoughts and ambitions, to His heavenly Father. He enjoyed going to church — as His ancestor David had — and He delighted in His conversations with God.

This became very obvious when He stayed behind in Jerusalem at the age of twelve. Mary and Joseph worried about His absence. But what a desirable kind of worry for parents to suffer!

What parents would not exchange this kind of worry for that which is caused by delinquency and rebellion? The hunger for God's Word in the case of Jesus was fed with the promises of God and with the strength to love.

Parents also can take a lesson from this incident. They can remember that their children are individuals and that as teenagers they must be readied for responsibility and trust and encouraged to act on their religious convictions.

Have your children tell you — after a visit to church or Sunday school — what they liked the most about their study and worship. If they have negative feelings, let them feel free to express them, and together with them examine how you might together look for values in worship you may have been missing.

And thank God, with relief, for the curiosity your child has about the things of his heavenly Father.

THE EDITOR

Jon and the Little Lost Lamb

LUKE 15:1-7 FOR CHILDREN

Written by Jane Latourette

Illustrated by Betty Wind

ARCH Books

© 1965 CONCORDIA PUBLISHING HOUSE, ST. LOUIS, MISSOURI

LIBRARY OF CONGRESS CATALOG CARD NO. 65-15145
MANUFACTURED IN THE UNITED STATES OF AMERICA
ISBN 0-570-06008-7

Inside the sheepfold, fast asleep,
What do you see? One hundred sheep!
That little one is "Baby Baa,"
who loves to snuggle in a heap
beside his brothers on the straw.

The morning sun is peeking in
to waken Baby Baa, who's been
a-dreaming of the meadow grass
that grows up where the hills begin,
right near the narrow mountain pass.

Since now another day's begun,
who comes along but Jonathan,
the shepherd, who unlocks the door,
and counts each sheep to see that none
is missing or is sick or sore?

One hundred strong, all safe and sound,
come greet the sun, as out they bound.
And little Baby Baa runs, too,
his tiny hoofs beat on the ground —
until he spies a plant to chew.

The shepherd lets them frisk and play,
before he leads them on their way
to meadows green, quite far from home —
good Jonathan knows every day
just where it's best to graze and roam.

At times it can be dangerous,
    as through the narrow mountain pas[s]
    they walk along in single file—

(Now, Baa, don't be so *mis*chievous!)
so Jon is watching all the while
to see that wolves aren't waiting there
about to spring down from their lair.

What's that? A lion sees the flock!
The shepherd, with no time to spare,
hurls with his sling a well-aimed rock.

He hits the beast between the eyes.
The lion falls. Stone-still he lies;
he's harmless now. Say, look ahead —
green, juicy grass! Their spirits rise,
and as they eat, Jon has his bread.

His kindly eyes keep in full view
his flock of sheep, who romp and chew,
or rest beneath the big tree's shade.
Let's see what Jon's about to do —
sweet music on the flute he made!

The hours go by, the sun sinks low;
it must be time for them to go
along the path for home again.
The shepherd calls, and in a row
he leads them downhill toward their pen.

They reach the fold; the shepherd counts
the sheep as through the door they bounce
to find a soft spot on the straw.
But wait! Just ninety-nine? He frowns —
oh, *where* is little Baby Baa?

How sad is our good shepherd Jon;
one lamb is lost or strayed. It's gone.
Jon's tired from tending sheep all day —
but he must search up hill and down
and find this lamb who's lost his way.

Jon climbs back to the pasture ground,
keeps calling, looking all around —
until beyond the place they'd stayed
he hears a little bleat that sounds
so low and faint and sore afraid.

You see, this lamb forgot and strayed
from his good shepherd late that day
He did not hear Jon's call to come
and get in line for walking home,
so Baby Baa just romped and played.

But then he stumbled, tumbled down
into a hole — Would he be found?
The day turned slowly into night;
no shepherd near. What was that sound?
A jackal's howl — Baa froze with fright.

Another sound — his shepherd's voice!
Above the wild beast's night-time noise.
Baa's gently lifted up by Jon;
what happy reason to rejoice!
So safe at last, all fear is gone.

Once back inside the snug sheepfold,
the shepherd does not rant nor scold,
but smooths on olive oil to heal

all Baa's deep scratches, and we're told
it's done so kindly, Baa can feel
How much his shepherd cares for him —
one poor, lost lamb, back home again!

Dear Parents:

Our story is based on Jesus' parable of the Lost Sheep, a companion-story to His parables of the Lost Son and Lost Coin. All of these stories were told by Jesus to explain why He bothered about lost men. (Luke 15:1, 2)

"My attitude is like that of a good shepherd," Jesus says in this parable. God's feelings are just like the shepherd's: he is not satisfied with still having the "ninety-nine." The lostness of the one sheep does not let him rest. His joy over finding a stray sheep is even greater than any satisfaction over his having many sheep who are not lost.

Will you help your child see that Jesus is like the shepherd of our story? That He cares about and loves all God's children, even those who have been bad? That He does not leave them, nor does He want *us* to leave them, to their foolishness but rather brings them back home with joy? He is the "good shepherd Jonathan."

                                                THE EDITOR

The Day the Little Children Came

Matthew 19:13-15 FOR CHILDREN

Written by Anne Jennings

Illustrated by John D. Firestone & Associates

ARCH Books

COPYRIGHT © 1975 CONCORDIA PUBLISHING HOUSE, ST. LOUIS, MISSOURI

MANUFACTURED IN THE UNITED STATES OF AMERICA

ISBN 0-570-06092-3

Concordia
Publishing House
St. Louis

My name is John, and I am a
    Disciple of the Man
Whose fame is spreading everywhere.
    I'm learning all I can
Of friendship, happy brotherhood,
    Of love both strong and sure,
Sent by our Heavenly Father
    To bless both rich and poor.

The Man, so cherished and admired,
Is often worn and very tired,
But not too much so, I have learned,
    A kindly deed to do.
The happening I shall describe
    Will prove that this is true.
I call it by a simple name:
"The Day the Little Children Came."

It was quite warm. The Master sat
    Beneath a cedar tree.
He'd closed His eyes; we knew that He
    Was weary as could be.
We spoke in faintest whispers then
    And softly did we walk,
Well knowing we must wake Him when
    'Twas time for Him to talk.

I noted all the people then:
Women, young children, tall bronzed men,
A darkskinned Ethiopian,
His little daughter too,
An Oriental with a child,
And many a bearded Jew.

One Jewish child I did admire;
His eyes were glowing dusky fire.
Now Peter, a disciple too,
    Exchanged a look with me.

We said to the assembled crowd,
   "Please let the Master be.
Pray call your children back to you
   That He may rest a while."
The children stood, uncertainly.
   I saw the Master smile.

His voice rose clearly on that day,
And suddenly I heard Him say:
"Let the small children come to Me,
    And do not you forbid them.
The Heavenly Father, loving all,
    Beneath His wing has hid them.
The paths the children's feet have trod
Are but the paths that lead to God.

"Go to the Man, and speak to Him,
        My daughter," Father said.
The Stranger smiled and laid His hand
        So gently on my head.
I found myself a-telling Him,
        Without a trace of fear:
"I'm Myrl, from Ethiopia,
        And I was eight this year.

We've come today to hear You speak."
He nodded. Then he touched my cheek.
"Well, Myrl from Ethiopia,
    Is something on your mind?"
I said, "Please help me, if You can,
    The way to God to find."
The Stranger spoke so lovingly.
"You've chosen the right way," said He.

I'd traveled with the caravan
    For many a weary day.
My uncle spoke. "Well, young Ho Feng,
    We've come an endless way
To hear the Man of whom all speak,
    Of whom such tales are told.
Tell Him you're from the Orient
    And that you're eight years old."

I laid my small thoughts like a band
Of beads into the Stranger's hand.
"It's kind of You to hear me now.
        A listener," I said,
"Is what I need above all things,
        Because my father's dead."

The Stranger spoke, so very clearly:
"Your Father, Ho Feng, loves you dearly."

My father took me by the hand
 And led me to the Man.
"This is Joel, just nine," he said.
 "Pray help him if You can.
In market place and synagogue
 We hear Your holy name;
Wherever Jewish people meet,
 One learns about Your fame."

The great Man smiled and questioned, "Well,
Are you a happy boy, Joel?"
"I have no brother and, alas!
    No sister," then I cried.
"I'm often very lonely, Sir."
    "I know," the Man replied,
"That loneliness is hard to bear.
We'll find you brothers, everywhere!"

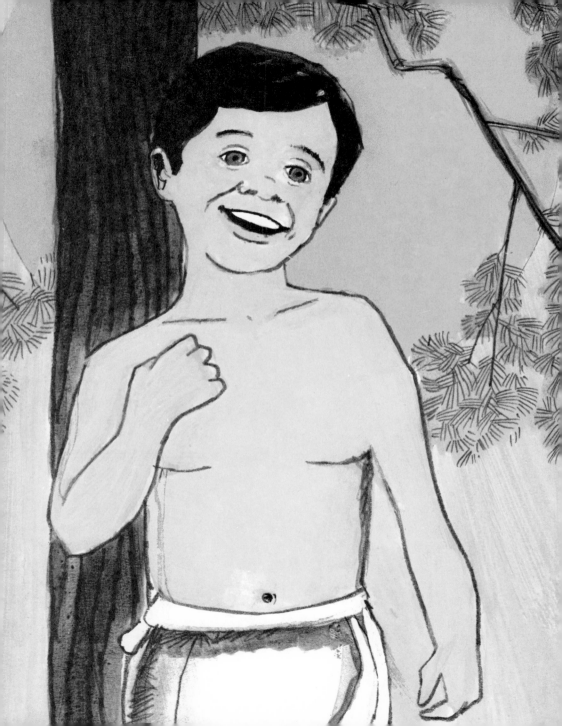

"Who would receive God's kingdom now,"
    Jesus said—His voice was mild—
"Must do so as the children here,
    Become a little child."
And then He blessed the children all,
    Among them, it is true.
The darkskinned Ethiopian,
    The Oriental too,
The Jewish child with dusky eyes—
His word to each was kind and wise:

"The way to God's through Me, young Myrl.
　　You, Oriental boy,
Your Heavenly Father loves you well;
　　He is your hope and joy."
His gesture took in all the others:
"Joel, all are sisters, all are brothers!"
A quiet lay upon the group,
　　Soft as a velvet glove.
We'd learned a lesson on that day
　　Of kindness, truth, and love.

The lesson I shall not forget.
I see it all so clearly yet.
Each episode I still can name,
The day the little children came.

DEAR PARENTS:

We don't really know very much about the children who came to Jesus to be blessed, except for the fact that they were real children with real feelings and concerns — in fact, not so very different from the children who come to Jesus today. And we know one other thing about them: that Jesus *wanted* them to come to Him, that He loved and blessed them. That's no different today either.

Help your children understand that they can come to Jesus just as Myrl and Ho Feng and Joel did. They can tell Him their troubles and share with Him their joys. He doesn't want anything or anyone to stand in their way; He wants to talk with *them*. And just as those children in long-ago Bible times, your children can be certain of His response to them, of His love and His blessing.

THE EDITOR

The Boy Who Gave His Lunch Away

JOHN 6:1-15 FOR CHILDREN

Written by
Dave Hill

Illustrated by
Betty Wind

RCH Books

1967 CONCORDIA PUBLISHING HOUSE, ST. LOUIS, MISSOURI

NUFACTURED IN THE UNITED STATES OF AMERICA
RIGHTS RESERVED
N 0-570-06027-3

Joel lived a happy life
down by Lake Galilee.
"We have a farm," he liked to say,
"for Mom and Dad and me."

His dad grew barley, oats, and wheat
for baking rolls and bread.
"What we don't eat we give away,"
was what he always said.

Joel knew what Father meant,
for EVERYONE needs bread.
"But why are some folks poor," he asked,
"when we are so well fed?"

"It isn't fair at all, I know,
but someday," Father said,
"the good Messiah will be here,
and He will be our King.
Then there will be no rich or poor.
We'll all have everything!"

So Joel helped his folks at work.
He rose each day at four
and washed the pots and scrubbed the pans
and swept and mopped the floor.
He helped his dad fill up the bags
of bread to give the poor.

One warm June day a neighbor stopped
to buy a loaf of bread.
"I'm on my way to see the King.
He's right nearby," he said.

"A king?" said Joel.
"Right nearby?
You must be fooling me!"
The stranger shook his head.
"I'm not!
Why, people say that He
is God's Messiah – here at last!
Why don't you come and see?"

"Is this the man named Jesus, sir?"
asked Father with a smile.
"Because, if so, my son can go
and see Him for a while."

"The very man!" the neighbor cried.
"You've heard of Him, I see!"

"I've heard He's kind and loves the Lord.
That's good enough for me!"

"You'd better take
this lunch along,
my boy," his mother said.
"I've packed you up
two fish and five
small loaves of
barley bread."

"I won't need that!" cried Joel. "Why, the King will feed the poor!"

But Father told him, "Take it, son," as they went out the door.

So up the road, with lu
the two went with a sm
They soon came to a n
stretched out for half a
"He must be near! We'l
in just a little while!"

in hand,

crowd
e.

the King

"That's Jesus there!"
a voice called out,
and Joel turned to see.
There stood a man
as plain and poor
as any man could be!

He ran up close
where he could see,
and hear what Jesus said.
"Is this the King —
this plain, poor man?
I'm glad I brought
some bread!"

Then Jesus spoke; His voice was strong:
"Bring all the sick to Me!"
And Joel stared as lame folks walked
and blind men cried: "I see!"

As Joel watched, he saw the sick
made whole and well and strong.
"Our King! Our King!" a shout rose up
from all who came along.

Then Jesus turned
and raised a hand
and spoke out
loud and clear:
"The kingdom that
God promised you
you see
already here!

"The kingdom
the Messiah brings
is full of
love and joy.
It's like a happy
dinner that
a king gives
for his boy."

The day grew short, and someone cried:
"I wish we had some bread!"
A man beside the Teacher spoke:
"How will these folks be fed?"

When Joel heard, he ran right up:
"I have some bread and fish.
I'll gladly share them with the crowd
if that is what you wish!"

"Five loaves? Two fish? For all this mob?"
asked one man with a frown.
But Jesus took the food and said,
"Have everyone sit down."

"We thank you, Father," Jesus prayed
and blessed and broke the bread.
Then His disciples passed it out
till ALL THE CROWD was fed.

"A miracle!" somebody cried.
"There's food for all to share!"
The helpers even gathered up
twelve baskets full to spare.

"Hooray! Hooray!" the people cheered.
"Shall we crown Jesus king?
He'll always give us what we need,
and we'll have everything!"
But Jesus turned and hurried off.
He wanted no such thing!

DEAR PARENTS:

Like Joel, people in New Testament times looked for the promised Messiah to come and establish His kingdom. In their deep longing they hoped for a time when the hungry would have enough to eat and the poor would have all their needs supplied.

In Jesus, the Messiah, the kingdom of God came according to promise. Jesus announced the Kingdom in words: "The time is fulfilled, and the kingdom of God is at hand" (Mark 1:15). He performed many signs to indicate the coming of God's kingdom, or gracious rule, over men. The feeding of the 5,000 with five loaves and two fishes is such a sign. This feeding miracle reminds us of parables in which Jesus compared the kingdom of God to a great dinner banquet. He invites all people, good and bad, rich and poor. God provides for the needs of people in generous abundance at this banquet. There is plenty for all, even when our faith is too small to see how God can provide. Resources at the banquet may be limited, but Christ uses them to feed the thousands who come to Him.

The people who were fed by the loaves and fishes were impressed by Jesus' powers. They wanted to make Him a bread king to satisfy their hunger and other needs of daily life. Because they misunderstood the King and His kingdom, "Jesus withdrew again to the hills by Himself" (John 6:15). He is more than a supplier of free bread. He is the "Bread of Life" (John 6:35), who brings the rule of God to us and gives us His goodness and love.

Will you help your child see the meaning of our story as the work of Christ putting God's kingdom into action? Will you help him experience the joy and abundance of life in Christ's church?

THE EDITOR

the little
Sleeping Beauty

LUKE 8:40-42, 49-56 FOR CHILDREN

Written by Brenda Grace Prior

Illustrated by Alice Hausner

ARCH Books
© 1969 CONCORDIA PUBLISHING HOUSE, ST. LOUIS, MISSOURI

MANUFACTURED IN THE UNITED STATES OF AMERICA
ISBN-0-570-06041-9

One day at sunrise,
when the moon had faded
and the brown hills were
turned to gold,

a little boat came bobbing
across the shining Sea of Galilee.

And on the shore
a crowd of people,
like a rushing tide,
ran down to welcome Jesus.

Many of them were poor
and many old and sick;
barefoot beggars dressed in rags,
and noisy children
pushing and shoving the fine ladies,
stepping on the toes of wealthy merchants,
craning their necks
to see the quiet Man
whose face was turned to greet them
and whose eyes were full of pity.

And Jesus, standing tall
among His robed disciples,
stretched out His gentle hands to heal
the blind, the sick, the lame.

Then
suddenly
pushing his way
through the crowd,
came a well-dressed man,
Jairus, president of a Jewish church,
a great man, known to all.
The people, bowing, stood aside to let him pa

Then Jairus, in his splendid robes,
knelt down in the dust
at the feet of Jesus.

"Master," he said, "my little girl,
my only child, is ill,
and if You do not come at once
and heal her,
she will surely die."

As he spoke, his face
was wrinkled up with grief.

So Jesus went with Jairus,
and the people followed
to see what He would do.

But as they walked along
the dry, hard path
beside the deep-blue sea,

a man came to tell Jairus
that his little girl was dead
and there was no need
to trouble Jesus anymore.

But Jesus said,
"Have no fear; only have faith.
She will be well."
And taking His friends
Peter, James, and John,
He followed Jairus to the big, white house
shaded by palm trees from the noonday sun.

Everyone was crying and wailing.
The mother was sobbing.

Her little girl would be there no more
to play in the bright garden, singing like a
bird beside the silver fountain.

The tall, white-robed Stranger,
without so much as looking at the child,
said calmly, "Do not weep.
The little girl's not dead; she is asleep."

"Asleep!" the people laughed.
As if the doctors did not know
better than He!

But
Jesus
sent
them
all
outside.

Then, with the parents at His side
and His three friends following,
He went into the low, cool room
where the little maiden lay.

"My child," He said
and gently took her hand,
"I say to you,
Arise!"

And the little girl sat up,
then danced around the room
and kissed her parents,
who were crying now for joy.

Then Jesus said, "Give her some food."

He asked Jairus and his wife
to tell no one
what He had done.

But others knew and told.
And many people heard
how Jesus brought the little girl to life
to play and sing again
around the silver fountain
in her happy parents' garden.

DEAR PARENTS:

Death is a sorrowful experience, but the death of a child causes the deepest sense of grief and loss. It seems cruel and senseless to see a beautiful child die of a painful disease or in an accident. Our civilization has tried to cover the ugliness of death with flowers, cosmetics, and caskets, but the reality of death cannot be hidden, especially from a child.

Because Adam sinned, death came into the world and has spread to all men, as Paul says in Romans 5:12. The Scriptures do not try to hide death or make it pretty; they take death seriously. Death is real.

But life is real too, and the victory over death is real. God became man and lived among us. Jesus Christ, the Son of God, died in our place. By His resurrection He overcame death for us.

Even before His own resurrection Jesus revealed His power over death by restoring life to the 12-year-old daughter of Jairus. The father of the "Little Sleeping Beauty" believed that Jesus was the strong Son of God who could help.

You can help your child understand death by answering his questions honestly. More important, you can give your child hope as you share your faith in the living Christ, who overcame death and will raise you from death to everlasting life.

THE EDITOR